IN TRANSIT
POEMS OF TRAVEL

OTHER TITLES FROM THE EMMA PRESS

POETRY ANTHOLOGIES

This Is Not Your Final Form: Poems about Birmingham
The Emma Press Anthology of Aunts
The Emma Press Anthology of Love
Some Cannot Be Caught: The Emma Press Book of Beasts

BOOKS FOR CHILDREN

Moon Juice, by Kate Wakeling
The Noisy Classroom, by Ieva Flamingo
Queen of Seagulls, by Rūta Briede
The Book of Clouds, by Juris Kronbergs

PROSE PAMPHLETS

Postcard Stories, by Jan Carson
First fox, by Leanne Radojkovich
The Secret Box, by Daina Tabūna
Me and My Cameras, by Malachi O'Doherty

POETRY PAMPHLETS

Dragonish, by Emma Simon
Pisanki, by Zosia Kuczyńska
Who Seemed Alive & Altogether Real, by Padraig Regan
Paisley, by Rakhshan Rizwan

THE EMMA PRESS PICKS

The Dragon and The Bomb, by Andrew Wynn Owen
Meat Songs, by Jack Nicholls
Birmingham Jazz Incarnation, by Simon Turner
Bezdelki, by Carol Rumens

In Transit
POEMS OF TRAVEL
Edited by Sarah Jackson
and Tim Youngs

THE EMMA PRESS

First published in Great Britain in 2018 by the Emma Press Ltd

Poems copyright © individual copyright holders 2018
Selection copyright © Sarah Jackson and Tim Youngs 2018

All rights reserved.

The right of Sarah Jackson and Tim Youngs to be identified as the editors of this work has been asserted by them in accordance with the Copyright, Designs and Patents Act 1988.

ISBN 978-1-910139-94-3

A CIP catalogue record of this book
is available from the British Library.

Printed and bound in Great Britain
by TJ International, Padstow.

The Emma Press
theemmapress.com
queries@theemmapress.com
Jewellery Quarter, Birmingham, UK

EDITORS' FOREWORD

There, through the last of the sentences, just there—
through the last of the sentences, the road—
    —Carolyn Forché, 'Travel Papers' (2011)

Whether they are local or global, made by foot or by ferry, we tend to look upon journeys in terms of departure and arrival. However much we enjoy or endure it, travel is often understood simply as a means of getting from one place to another. But what happens en route? Do journeys change or confirm us? And what happens when we are forced to travel, or when we have no choice but to stay put? These questions are at the heart of this anthology. Whatever the scale of the journey, whether international or close to home, the poems in this collection explore the experience of being in transit.

Travel writing is usually thought of as a prose genre, yet the relationship between poetry and travel is deep and ancient. From Homer's *The Odyssey* to Dr. Seuss's 'Oh, The Places You'll Go', movement is inherent in poetic form. As others have noted, the word 'verse' has its etymological roots in the turn of the plough; 'stanza' is a station or stopping-place. Metre is employed to convey not only the rhythms of breath and speech but also those of motion. Punctuation controls the pace of reading and the location and duration of the pause; rhyme returns us. Poems reshape the journey and are uniquely able to move through time and place in a compressed space.

In our call for this anthology, which is a collaboration between the Emma Press and Nottingham Trent University's

Centre for Travel Writing Studies, we asked for contributions that dealt with the experience of being in transit. We were especially interested in how the fact of being in motion affects our sense of identity, our relationship with others, and our perspective on our surroundings. We wanted to see how the mode of transport impacts on these factors and how it might influence the shape as well as the content of each poem.

Trains were by far the most popular means of transport in our submissions, followed by aeroplanes and then boats. There were walks, though fewer than we expected. Bicycles and motorcycles, buses and trams scarcely figured. We were surprised by how very little the car featured, considering its status as probably the most common form of mechanised transport in the industrialised West.

Several of the poems are set in the speaker's destination but show that the journey continues long after arrival. Whatever the setting, the mode or the scale of the journey, these poems demonstrate how physical travel can open up new ways of perceiving, relating, thinking and feeling. Undertaken for reasons of leisure, work, family, forced exile or willed migration, movement reflects and helps constitute who we are.

The journey undergoes a further transition, of course, when it is crafted for the page. Whether in traditional form or in free verse, epiphanic or wholly mundane, the poetic treatment of travel both continues and recrafts it, as does each reading.

SARAH JACKSON AND TIM YOUNGS
APRIL 2018

CONTENTS

Vantage point, by Susannah Hart 1
Always pleasing this quarter sun, by Lila Matsumoto 2
Beijing, by David Tait 3
Catherine spread the map on the bed, by Miranda Peake ... 4
Japeth's stuff, by William Roychowdhury 6
Sleeper, by Rory Waterman 7
Balloonist, by Peter Surkov 8
Family Reunion, March 2001, by Zayneb Allak 9
Walnuts, by Rich Goodson 12
Short Stay, by Susannah Hart 13
Square Dancing the Adriatic, by Colleen J. McElroy 14
South, by Zayneb Allak 18
Creeks and Culverts of New Zealand, by Ilse Pedler 19
Taverna, by Jane McKie 20
Alligator, by Anna Kisby 23
The Girls from Maynard's, by Nick Littler 24
The Long Flight Home, by Shara Lessley 26
Travelling on the 10.21 with Tom Hardy, by Maria Taylor 28
[Watford Gap], by Andrew Taylor 29

Postcard, by Fiona Moore 31
West Highland, by Sharon Black 32
Empty Quarter, by Rosie Garland 33
The Sight to See, by Colleen J. McElroy 34
France, by Miranda Peake 36
Halfway to Voronezh, by Charlotte Eichler 39
Train to Cambridge, by Jeremy Wikeley 40
Epicentres, by Rory Waterman 41
The romance of men in boats, by Miranda Peake 42
Reading the Water, by Nancy Campbell 44
Quayside, by Rich Goodson 45
Men in Water, by Andy Eaton 47
Herring Gurl, by Rebecca Violet White 48
Aboard the Grey Ghost, by Simon Williams 50
Чайка, by Alex Toms 51
Stopper on the Poacher Line, by Jo Dixon 53
Dual Gauge, by Vicky Sparrow 54
Copenhagen to Stockholm, by Cliff Yates 57
Georg Rides the U-Bahn, by Fiona Larkin 58
Thirty-Eight Thousand Feet, by Claire Collison 59
Red-eye, by Cheryl Pearson 61
The Crow and the Dove Take Your Shape, by Anna Kisby ...
.... 62
Uptown, by Jeanette Burton 63

Walking, by Baiba Bičole 65

Portrait of my father as Joseph Cornell, by Andrea Robinson 66

Return, by Rebecca Gethin 68

If You Lived Here You'd Be Home By Now, by David Tait 69

The Blue, by David Tait 70

In Dyeliva, by Peter Surkov 72

La Pive, by Yvonne Reddick 74

Gods, Cabo de São Vicente, Portugal, by Jane McKie 75

Little Blue Truck, by George David Clark 76

☙

Acknowledgements 79
About the editors 80
About the authors 80

Vantage point

Impossible these days to believe in the sky,
the way it dissipates on contact,
its vanishing trick.

Believe rather in the bas-relief below,
in the scarcely visible contour lines
mapping the hills.

Believe in the lights, frangible
and scattered, where they've been
intemperately thrown,

or believe in the gardens hardening
into February, the curvature of the mist,
the promising roads.

LILA MATSUMOTO

Always pleasing this quarter sun

Trains follow trails as hands do, on a rail, in the dark.
Or an eagle poised to hunt dogs, its eye distilled to a
point cresting the hill. A man carrying a sack is reaching
for a grape.

What kind of day is this? What moment? Pane shows clover
rushing, so fast the rushing is still. Pane is cool against cheek.

A pebble a romantic a shovel a branch a trough before a rose
a line in a box. Tan, peat, a wood scarred fauve. Fronds.
They take note of the passing.

Greenness a carpet grows is pressed as a rose or a sweet pea.

All attention is here where bursting is good, is good.
Choosing fast in foam and ash. The bright souvenir
expanding, a moment disinterred –

Beijing

Whenever I'm landing in this city
I'm reminded of the x-rays of my grandfather's chest.

I look down at the roads and remember his ribs,
and passing through the smoggy forcefield

I think about the clouded part above his heart,
and the pain that brought him, proud, to the hospital.

Sometimes in this city of pylons and pagodas
we catch a snatch of blue, fresh air after a typhoon,

and we join the crowds that walk by the river,
all stuffing ourselves full of good air, as if at a buffet.

Catherine spread the map on the bed

Charles folded himself twice to see and said look, it's there,
no hang on, that's the Philippines, it's here!

Bent double, their mouths filled with the taste, unsteady
and sea-sick, syllables swallowed down and brought back up

until they got to grips with it. They knew a boat
would take them there but didn't really know until their feet

were on the deck how it would feel to see the green
eaten by the blue. Because everything was new it didn't matter

and there was her body, how it stretched around a tiny boy –
Michael, but he was hard to come by and almost didn't stay.

The doctors said ポリオ, though later they said other things.
To her they said 腸チフス, and rest, Catherine, rest.

Charles stood in the centre of the room, arms outstretched
and said beloved, I'm sorry, for bringing us to this.

From her bed, Catherine could see the cherry blossom
was in bloom and she said darling look!

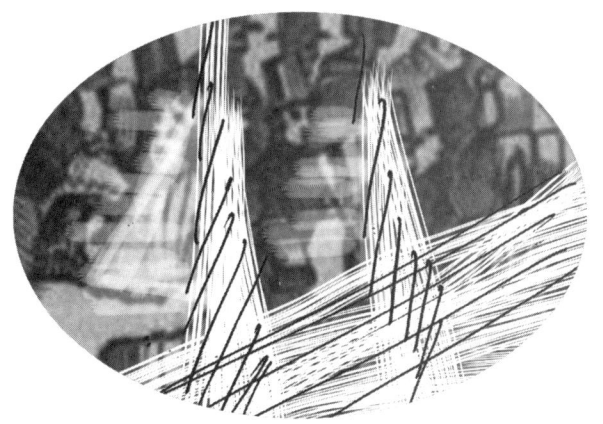

WILLIAM ROYCHOWDHURY

Japeth's stuff

So I'm like *Dad I need time to pack my stuff* and he's
you've got 24 hours
till then it wasn't real   I mean what even is gopher-wood

him building it that April long in the back garden
watching for the crackle in a tinfoil sky
and Mum with her looks like
rain about to leave him   like they said she should

it was hard to get the pool table up the gangplank
what with all the llamas   and shit   then the living
   quarters were just rank
no room for my sounds or my plasma TV
Dad said they'd clear some space   that's love

I remember on the prow some displaced rhino standing still
like an inkblot from the sky if the sky
wrote in iron
               and how Mum tipped
                    a crate of butterflies   like red tea
                                        into the sea

By the time we cast off through the melting caps my side
   listed
and all our packed up world   lolled   high   like a
   harpooned   whale
a bleed of macaw along the hull
while Dad just looked sad with his biblical eyes
watching me like it was all a metaphor or something

Sleeper

You sat askance in a taxi, jolting past rush hour,
then took the sleeper home to watch your nana –
her tight mouth sunk in shrunk surprise
still, though now her eyes were shut and breath,
not how she knew you, was all she'd battle for.

Bolting past coast then cornfields, through dusk then dark
you saw it all, then filled the flip-down berth.
And stitching your in-out sleep, the wheels battered on
sending their morse over towns, under trees, along cuttings.

Balloonist

The passengers are only ballast.
Flight's purpose
is other than payment.

On touchdown, my lips
are untouched by champagne.
My business is flame, rope,
and lift of fattened silk.

ZAYNEB ALLAK

Family Reunion, March 2001

I. Baghdad

There was fresh sunshine every morning
and squeezed orange juice in a jug

when I woke up. My grandmother was tiny
and it was funny. The last time I'd seen her

I'd been tinier still. There were other tiny things,
like glasses full of red tea and mini cucumbers

that were sweet. One time my cousin made me laugh
so much I gagged. When I bit the air I bit fear.

One time the president's face stayed on the screen
for so long I thought the television was broken.

On the day we said goodbye I cried
for all the tiny things. At the side of the road

the rubbish had grown, uncollected.
There was a bribe and a theft as we crossed

the border. At Heathrow my dad and I
joined the queue for EU and UK Nationals Only.

We wiggled our eyebrows and kissed our passports.
My dad said his back hurt from the flight

but he leaned into the trolley
and I ran after him as he rode it down the ramp.

ii. LONDON

Alone that night in the empty terminal
I waited two hours for the cab driver to come.

As he drove he asked me where had I been
and who had I seen. He said

he had worked in construction in Baghdad,
back in the eighties. In the rear-view mirror

our eyes caught. He coughed. We didn't speak,
blinked apart. Orange lights streaked

until we got to Brixton. His mistake was
that thing about construction.

In his place I would've acted friendlier,
more surprised. I would've said, Baghdad?

A young woman like you?
Or stopped the cab to find my real eyes and state:

at this time of terrorist threat it is imperative
that we monitor all suspect travel to and from Iraq.

Either way, I would've answered him: I will tell you
how it appeared to me. People had fear

like a rolled-up rag rammed in their mouths.
If I were in his place, so as not to blow my cover,

I would've asked questions about the route home, double-
checked on the best course. I would not have driven

left, right, left, right without
doubt all the way up to my front door.

Walnuts

Sure, my passport's British, my passport's kosher –
but if they find the bag of walnuts in my carry-on –

Yes, Officer. The green stain in my palm's because I picked them myself.

Yes, Officer. Each one's a fossilised monkeybrain still in its skull –

The walnuts are growing – with each step toward Airport Security,
across these polished-mirror floors –
increasingly X-rayable.

But they're clean. They're hairless. They're free of disease.
Shelled or unshelled, they're not IEDs.

I slide my thumbnail under the plexiglass.

What will they divine
in my blush-response?

My genome is
61% German,
19% Norwegian,
19% Irish
&
1% Neanderthal.

I'm obese with identities.

Short Stay

Dimensions are stretched here, beyond 4th and 5th,
spatial and temporal overlapping. The control tower
is at once Berlin Alexanderplatz and Magaluf,
the spy coming in from the cold and raffia donkeys
stacked up in the souvenir shops, all those ways
you remember where you've been and what you thought
it meant. It occurs to you that perhaps all people
can be divided into plants and birds, the tethered
and the rootless, the rhizomed and the floating free.
Babies don't know if they'll grow feathers or root hairs,
just as you don't know if you'll join the queue for check-in
or turn tail past the concrete and the lift shafts,
where the smell of fuel hovers like the machinery of deceit.

COLLEEN J. McELROY

Square Dancing the Adriatic

no matter how you cut
it you can't get
there   from
                              here   grab a train   a bus
                                              a plane   grab a boat
                                              anything that moves
                              grab
a hint   of Black
descendants in a town
called Ulcinj – hidden
naturally in back of
this ragged backwater
country full of Turks
and other unseemingly   dark
                        folks   take that road,   left
                                        the right fork,   turn
                                        lady, you   are
                        for
                        sure
                        lost!
listen to Dubrovnik
rug merchants [that's
the trick and   those
                        dudes
                        have   all the clues]   never
                                       mind if they speak
                                       without breaking a
                                       flirt, honey

                              this
                              story

earns a history of
dinners back on home
turf   :hire
                              a car   – some dashing Slav
                                                on his first time out
                                                who will drive break
                                                neck roads at night
                                                with no headlights –
                                                forget those ditches
                                                filled with rotting
                                                hulks of
                              tour
                              busses
stay off the bus stay
off the boat don't
walk   the end is
near – get it? – no
sweat: danger is   your
                              middle
                              name   now enter   Medjugorje
                                                town of ugly pilgrims
                                                watching pretty
                                                virgins high on wheat
                                                germ and boredom
                                                pray for the real
                                                Mary to star in their
                                                tv road show

                        babe you
                        best get
                        out
while you have
someplace to go – draw
a line from your head
to the nearest border   – ask   the gypsy on the
                                          corner – she knows a
                                          Greek driver who has
                                          been here before

                        you can
                        awaken
in Albania groaning
through Act Six of a
five hour King Lear
by gypsies – Kabuki
style – it never ends   get it?   so ignore   that sweet
                                          British critic beside
                                          you   he is a maniac
                                          for bleak landscapes
                                          and may keep you here

                        forever
unless you head for
the coast the path a
sheer drop from
cliffside to ocean
down to Adriatic surf   :follow   goats to the hut: 3rd
                                          from centre with some
                                          guy who's a caramel
                                          replica of your 2nd
                                          cousin's husband

                    [can't
                    you
                    remember?

– the cat who came
home from Chicago
with no teeth and
eight fingers!] but
now this *dragi*'s
talking to you –
and he's   like
                     suspicious   so use language you
                                       can muster – better
                                       make the accent
                                       Jamaican in case he
                                       hates
                     Americans
and don't slobber
he's kin, just a few
too many generations
removed – so don't
sweat it 'cause with next
                       year's
                       war   he'll hardly have
                                         time to remember your
                                         name – just give the
                                         high sign – say:
                                         Cheese
                       say:
Hi,   moj   Covjeck!
say: *Yeah,*
                       Soul   *Brother!*

South

> *The space of the foreigner is a moving train, a plane in flight, the very transition that precludes stopping.*
> —Julia Kristeva

I.

Another house tells me to leave.
The ceiling sags –
I climb the stairs to where it rains.

There's no way to fix this.
Water mulches the roof
and collapses the walls.

II.

On the train my eyes dart
but fields and buildings smudge.
I'm so tired I only hear in gulps.

I stumble along the train as it grinds
across the land. It carries me
south, towards a sea and sleep.

III.

Mites float, a mosquito zips, curtains are hazy.
Beyond the doors is a garden, hosed cool.
I'll borrow its shade and later

plant an orange tree and watch it grow
strong enough for me to climb
into its branches as they sway.

ILSE PEDLER

Creeks and Culverts of New Zealand

Granity Gully, Ribbonwood Creek, Palmerston Bridge:
they named them all; each creek, each culvert,
each tiny stream, marked with small yellow signs.

Some were obvious: the white cliffs rising above
White Cliff Breck, Heron Creek after the bird
that came those five summers past

and O'Rourke's Bridge, Fergusson's Gully after those
hard enduring men with calloused palms who worked
their acres, light glinting off the granite in their eyes.

I fancy it was women who named Rosie Stone Culvert
and Pretty Flower Creek, washing the pattern off
their dresses in water so cold their fingers burned

but what feats of strength were performed at Hercules Creek
and when they ran to Doctor's Gully with news of broken bones
and birthings did he come quickly, did they live?

I saw her standing at Disappointment Creek slowly
peeling bark from a twig and watching the pieces float away
and I looked on as the news they waited for at Little Hope Bridge

never came. We skim past in our campervan collecting names:
Eight Mile Creek, Nine Mile Creek, Ten Mile Creek

Taverna

In the green diamond where light splits the pines,
a shack buckles under its bold signage:

FULL ENGLISH BREAKFAST, GREEK COFFEE PLUS
ONE CIGARETTE, TRADITIONAL WOOD OVEN,
TONIGHT SPECIAL ONE GLASS OF SPARKLING WINE.

Year one

The walls sag, but nothing moves. A smoky
flavour on our tongues: the sun has died
and risen again and still nothing budges.
We customers are effigies, glasses in hands
propped up by the resinous bar, all asleep
under honey; we dream of asphodel flowers
and charred conversation. We dream
of coming here again next year.

Year two

You push the muted vermillion of raw meat
with your knife, your manner desolate,
mumbling like a vagrant. Don't court death.
Wait a moment. There will be delight to our hot,
Grecian romance; there will be lasting fit.

Year ten

You and I dissect fish with forks, under a pine tree,
watching the tines light up like matches struck
when branches shift. Talking is jaw-jaw, a play
where everything's been said. When we love, now,
it isn't love; it's drinks at four with old pals,
al fresco. Distant suns crawl towards their ends.
We're bombproof. What would it take to finish us off?

Alligator

We were driving through the bayou
when we passed signs warning *Alligator*.

The road we were driving was straight as fate
on a tarot card, waters rising on each side.

Driving together so long we were like one
person looking out for their Jurassic stares.

In those days not a soul knew where we were
and we went unrecorded except on reptile retinas.

Come this far south and nothing else to do
but pull into a layby in a fug of cicadas and love.

You never were a talker, held your cards close,
The Lovers in your palm dwarfed by a sun

warming the earth too fast. Two decades later
I hear alligators are in Virginia, heading for

the sewers of New York. Turns out they were
nothing special, nor us, nor the lightning bugs

glancing our windscreen as we sat close,
turning around and driving out of the wild

into the north and straight on into the bite
of the rest of our lives.

The Girls from Maynard's

They got the train from Central with some girls
from Maynard's who I didn't know. The world
was smaller then, and only stretched as far
as Chudleigh, where the party was that night,
so strangers from the girls' school, insofar
as they were different, seemed exotic – might
be up for it. We waited, drinking what
we'd smuggled from our parents' houses and
what those with badly-forged IDs had bought
from cornershops. After a while we handed
round some poppers. Still no news, and we
were getting antsy. Then the knock. And then
they all piled in, once Jack had turned the key.
And nothing ever felt the same again.
The boys cracked jokes, the girls just cried, and I
had nothing. When the train had stopped the guard
told them the cracking sound was branches. Mind,
it's windy out. It wasn't branches. Hard
and spiky shards of bone stuck out under
the wheels. The guard threw up outside. Wonder
if everybody else remembers it
the same. The poor girl all alone in bits.

SHARA LESSLEY

The Long Flight Home

Amman to Washington D.C.

Forget what I said about the black iris. I thought the national bird was the hawk. I expected mostly to touch something Holy, to see the Dead Sea scrolls locked in a temperature-regulated box. For years I toured the Cardo's sacred precinct,

totally clueless. When *pleasing* came out *Halloween*, the florist said *Speak English*. I'm still baffled by the military quartet bagpiping in the ruined temple. Don't ask me about the intifada. Don't ask who stashed the Russian ammunition in Irbid's tombs. There are

dissertations on why farmers turn bombers, why Bedouin adorn bridal caps with cowries and coins. Autumn reshuffled her cards. Arab Spring began that December; *First Noel*, blasting through the Palestinian bakery. Don't ask me why

thousands chanted support for the King while the Brotherhood made the papers. What do I think of His Majesty? They say he's the Prophet's descendant. They say he poses as a cabbie to glean what people think. Don't ask me whether I've prayed

in a taxi. I was mostly wrong about women. I was mistaken about men who deal arms. I've seen the High Altar of Sacrifice, doubt Salim was slain. Forget what I said about the maid locked in the apartment above us: I assumed her cries were

the wife's – some ordinary marital strife. Forget the sound in our common courtyard, white washcloths dropped like swifts. Her employers seized her passport, phone, held her wages. The national bird's a rosefinch; the national tree, a sub-

species of oak. One night, something like furniture breaking. I woke in a fog. Forget the sidewalk, the rail from which she leapt to the carport below. I expected to touch something holy. Her femur shattered, the x-ray would show. The chapter on

faith says not long ago it was custom horses tramp the backs of believers who lay in the street like dogs. It says distance clarifies misunderstanding. I'm told the human plank would hold.

Travelling on the 10.21 with Tom Hardy

Hardy calls to his dead wife
at Castle Boterel, St. Andrew's Tower.
He calls quietly over Wi-Fi,
Can it be you I hear?

Fields fly without answers.
A smudge of rabbit hops away
and vanishes into a grassy tuft.
A horse's silhouette awaits a rider.

My heart's a dog-eared *Metro*.
I hold my book under the table
as if I'm keeping his love a secret.
I am. We're both out of style

amid a one-upmanship of screens.
His simple question skims the roofs
of expanding towns. It pauses
over a clock's stopped hands.

[Watford Gap]

Watford Gap grass verge through coffee steam, reassurance of traffic noise, knowing we are an hour away – the beauty of the service station

Postcard

Three days and already I could write
a dissertation on the fastenings of gates:

the counterintuitive, industry standard
grey metal latch, to be clanged backwards;

the bolt with a spring that's always too strong;
the soft warmth of an old chain, brown stream

through fingers, binding the post with a hook;
the double gate's hard-edged central loop

with its guillotine rise/drop; and the frayed
Gordian knot of orange nylon twine, avoided

by climbing at the hinge end. Each one
a puzzle, each to be handled and worked on,

each gate lifted or pulled before I pass
from the last room of sheep or meadow flowers –

below hills that move up and down and up
as if walking their own walk –

to the next. With love.

West Highland

If I were to lie back, this is the landscape I'd become –
blanched tussocks, copses of pine,
shining lochs, station platform signs translated
to a language I can't pronounce;

lazy fences, serious houses, two shaggy rams
by a pleated auburn stream,
alder, beech and dithery aspen,
Munros shouldering the lost weight of snow;

a blaze of gorse along the verge, pylons marching
over bog and moor, the ninety-six miles we walked last year
with backache, slippery from sweat and midge spray,
the craic of good friends keeping us upright
as we lost and found our way.

Empty Quarter

On the eight-hour lorry ride from Al Fashir to Nyala, perched
on potato sacks, I am stripped of the constant bickering

of billboards and their one-upmanship of car, liquor,
sportswear, over and over. There are no other drivers

to tailgate, overtake, undertake, argue the noisy toss
with at red lights; no horns screaming at amber;

no beep of warnings to *wait, walk now, wait*
on street corners bunched into fists.

Parched grind as the truck shifts gear. The road unrolls.
All distractions swept off earth's table-top;

the only interruptions a shaved hill swelling
from pebbledash desert, a camel on the horizon,

paddling sand. An ochre moon advertises itself
against the night. I hear the breath of stars.

COLLEEN J. McELROY

The Sight to See

another country and faces that carry
reflections of cousins speaking
languages I've only imagined
another set of women with hips
legs   eyes like my mother's mother
skin polished by the same old sun

another harbour   another airport
and flight attendants with ready
trays of mystery food
another customs clerk
capricious as the weather
one more day cut by mountain ridges
glowing in various shades of purple

another line of bright-eyed children
and easy giggles   their grown-up
counterparts pocketing tips and maps
to lost places   promises of another
day of clocks turning backwards
and ladies wearing too much history

trapped in the tradition of mirrors
where like mama says: folks think
they looking cute but looking curious
another mirror surprised as I am
to find me here ignoring passing
comments on the verge of my origins

another moment where I grin
in the face of another meal
with too much or too little
another polite bowl of soup   strong
bread identified by salt or the hot
bite of peppers   another calendar
released at the border   another:
so long kiddo   welcome home sister –
girl, where've you been?

France

In the taxi from the airport
I tried to say
my friends are there already.
I tried to say
I'll need to get back again somehow.

>In the restaurant we remained English,
>suitcases at our feet.

He stopped for a wild boar dead
in the road. I arranged my face
for tragedy, but he
treated it like a lottery win.

>Arms loll towards glasses yellow
>to the top. Olives roll over and for a while
>everyone talks about the hornets,
>how they got into the kitchen,
>how we'll get them out.

I shift my legs to find a cool place
in the bed. From downstairs, female voices
insulate the house, chinking away
the things of dinner.

                    The men who are the most
                              like women,
                    those are the ones to choose
                    they said, spread about on sofas.

This room, big as a town square
holds the evening in,
slate grey
as alcohol starts to crumple my map.

CHARLOTTE EICHLER

Halfway to Voronezh

On a stopped train, sharing the chocolates
your fiancée gave you for the journey,
trying not to giggle as two men gut fish

on the table below, our carriage fills
with blood and sea. Through the window,
everything's blue, even the snow falling

on the forest – a map of this place
would have no names, only a dotted line
faint as breadcrumbs in the moonlight.

The stations we pass look temporary,
concrete platforms without signs;
unreal places that don't count.

When the heating breaks,
it only makes sense to share warmth.
The train pulls into the city on Sunday

and before you leave we get coffee,
watching twelve brides round a statue, posing
in varying shades of white.

JEREMY WIKELEY

Train to Cambridge

After Louis MacNeice

Beyond the window the sky is turning
pink and it's more surprising than in that
song I wrote about how surprised I was that
the sky was turning pink. It's turning

slowly, like it's enjoying itself, as if
there's no hurry. The evening is encouraging
the sky to follow it and the sky is following
in its own time, pink and pacing itself

while the train and I are racing to get ahead
of the turning of the world, only to find
that no matter how hard we try to push
ourselves we're always a sleeper behind

the evening as it strides along outside,
crushing the sun under its thumb, mixing
red dust with wet clouds and swiping
dark streaks across the cheeks of the sky.

Epicentres

St Denys' is making its stab for the Maker
and the 07:19 for Lincoln is rattling through its break
in the fields, then over a culvert, and on it you sit,
and look up from *Bizarre* straight through the view

where a church spire is flat on the whiteness of sky
with one dour gull shooting clear across its tip
and over the rain-bright roofs, cracked tarmac, then you,
and on to the coast where sharp groynes cut the breakers.

The romance of men in boats

overwhelms me on the water and I sway, quietly in love
with strangers, my suitcase wedged beneath my knees.

Repeated all across the slick of blue I see the three
of them forever leaning in, heads together as if to talk.

Occasionally a leg is lost, taken by lagoon, but even then
the balance holds, marking out the blue, as she stretches

all the way to where we're going. Confident, established,
no matter that she's not the sea, she's still spent every day

hiding it from me – the place where the blue of water meets
the blue of sky, until I realised I'd been wasting my time.

Who cares after all where one thing ends and another begins.

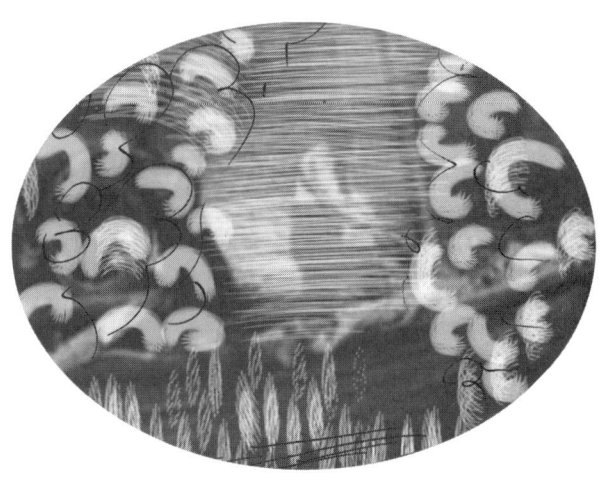

Reading the Water

Make the boy a kayak
from a speckled skin

let him hold a paddle
strap him safely in

take him to the shore
point the prow to sea

launch him in the shallows
and count to three.

Out of the darkness
seals will rise

to gauge their deaths
within his eyes.

They'll stare as if
he was one of their own

and dive back down
when you pull him home.

Quayside

Abdullah, fifteen, a Pashtun,
who'd have an AK47
ink-hammered the length of his forearm
if it wasn't haram,
strives to get online.

He sits in the gutter, knees to chin.
       A Greek Orthodox priest passes by on the other side.
He sits in the gutter, knees to chin.
       A tourist in a yellow bikini passes by on the other side.

For a signal he grips his phone against the sky.

On it are photos of his parents,
a barbecue in warm fields of wild rhubarb last June,
an address in Nottingham.

What's trickling down his arm? Is it sweat...? Milk...? Seawater...?

Yes, Driver. I'll do that thing for you.
Yes, Driver. I'll stay alive.

On the quayside, as he waits for the ferry to Piraeus, he thinks:
this phone this phone is all I own.

& my eyes
& my name

though his eyes – after all the long, dark days & long, dark nights
in the lorries from Kabul, & then the boat –
have become like stones

and his name's

been breaking
into breadcrumbs

in his throat.

Men in Water

I.

I know a man can feel at home at sea.

But in it two full nights, hanging
like a buoy above the deep
is a new story. We learn the way
a single body drifts from its ring
of others gathered round the raft,
the cold rubber. The quiet

laps against us, the cold moon's teeth.

II.

Of course, I did not notice it then
but you will have seen those photographs
of people wearing coloured suits in air

falling from a plane, holding hands,
a halo bound for earth – it was like that
without the suits, the thrill.

Herring Gurl

At this time of night at this time of year the roads have started to glitter
with ice glass, glass ice
and I am terrified of punctures in the teeth of the wind

Eyes sharp as the road, bill sharp as the road I have to crook my elbows back to take off
have to open the eyes so that they are full of the road turned grey
grey as the sea
grey as seals and whales slipping under the sky under the cliffs the colour of exposed bone
cliffs a tangle of nests, or dry grass and weed

Yellow beak parted I have to take in some of the sky as I go, skin glowing
face glistening like spilled egg white

This is when I scream, breathing the prickles of cold air and exhaling all of this joy

here I am, running down a hill almost never touching the ground

qua-qua-qua

here I am, now never touching the pavement qua

here I am, on wheels in winter, wings in winter

bright bike gurl

Aboard the Grey Ghost

Our steward says, 'The dolphins are back'
and I run to the prow with the others
and look over. Seven or eight of them
jumping where the sharp front cuts the sea.
Perhaps it's like a bubble bath for them.

This is the most fun since we left Southampton;
before that rain and bombs, Highgate
more smashed up every morning when we left the shelter,
until Mum said, 'We're leaving for Montana,
where your cousins live. Go and find it in the atlas.'

We've been aboard three days; one to go, the steward
says – perhaps the dolphins bring us luck.
We haven't seen a U-boat. The first
sign would be the scud of a torpedo
like a killer whale without the dorsal fin.

In the fog we've had to slow. Nothing's
out there, as if we're wiped off the world
or between two frames of film when
it gets jammed, just before the lamp
starts to blob and burn the celluloid.

Чайка*

After Valentina Tereshkova

Even as a child you longed for space:
a bird-girl climbing the cherry trees
that edged the field, free-falling
through a nebula of blossom
before crashing back down,
wearing your scabs like medals.

Years later you jumped from planes,
trusting in silk and the Motherland
that built factories and put men in space.
In those weightless moments when your stomach
caught up with your body, you wondered
if Gagarin had felt the same churning.

In '63 you clambered into Vostok 6
and made your final checks, safe
within your helmet's halo. Meanwhile,
your comrades at the factory lifted
their heads above the machinery's prayer
and wondered at your absence.

Your call signal was Чайка, and like a seagull
circling a trawler you girdled the earth.
You felt nauseous, but the world saw your smile
shine through TV's grey squall,
your voice almost a squawk –
ya chaika. I am a seagull –

and as you re-entered earth's atmosphere,
parachute blossoming,
you transformed from a seagull
into an *alkonost*: a gold plumed bird-woman
bearing a message from paradise
to the waiting people below.

* Чайка – Chaika

Stopper on the Poacher Line

leaving the platform buddleia, warehouses, vandal fences, mildewed swing-seats in back gardens, cerise plastic sheeting (hooked on dormant branches) flicking up and back like flamenco skirts

Fen-water gathering in ditches and near Great Hale Eau three cormorants displaying their wings to a sord of mallard napping on the bank, heads tucked in

caravans, a shipping container: off-grid breaking into fields bordering the Trent, fallstreaks from the clouds nudge the grass; two pheasants shoot up in a dash for fresh cover – racing, tails resisting air cerise plastic sheeting (hooked on dormant branches) flicking up and back like flamenco skirts, mildewed swing-seats in back gardens, vandal fences, warehouses, buddleia arriving at the platform

sand lodged in the tread of my boots, stomach still tight from the spectacle: indentations of flukes, whale tissue packed in polystyrene for the archive

Dual Gauge

> *Yet there isn't a train I wouldn't take,*
>   *No matter where it's going.*
>   —Edna St. Vincent Millay

Suitcase at my feet, I nudge forwards towards the perspex booth. I trouble the edges of my passport with my thumb. Travel documents are like commas, I think.

The filmmaker Werner Herzog walks from Munich to Paris to keep his friend alive. He knows that she will live until he arrives, so he walks. It is an act of full faith, of unreasonable reason, of keeping two lines apart.

To get to work I take a long train. The railway I use was built by migrant workers. In the motion of the train carriage, the mobility of the workers is monumentalised and reproduced.

This is the night train crossing the Border, dum diddi dum and the postal order. Auden's rhythm for the 'Night Mail' enacts as it describes. Somewhere between medium and message, it makes a world.

I fall hard into the luggage rack as the train jounces. A bruise in a straight line across my forearm will be platformed at the next station. Collapsed leakily, a suspicious item.

Marx says that goods become commodities on their way to market ['dieses örtliche Moment']: it is in their travel that they are valorised. I believe that sorcery. And it's the same for people, for we become objects on the road too.

Once for three months I was banned from entering the Borough of Westminster. I rerouted my bike, but never knew if I could take the tube beneath the borough. Subterranean meaning is indistinct.

'The art of travel is only a branch of the art of thinking', Wollstonecraft writes. Travel is a branch line in the going-somewhere of thought; poetry another. The tracks make familiar runnels.

I take a long haul flight once a year to the place my antecedents colonised not so very long ago. It is a source of shame. I plant my flag in the grey air it makes.

When asked what America was like, Stein said, 'conceive a space filled with moving'. Stein's repetition feels as if the word has moved, not as if it has been repeated. The same word moving.

Out of the train window, I can see things passing through the reflection of myself. (Which is always true.) I think how velocity shakes some people to pieces, and other people it stabilises.

Dickens' 'The Signal-Man' is about a premonition of someone's death causing their death. The signal travels the wrong way, so that death causes death. The signal actualises its meaning.

A novelist once took a line of my poetry. He told me he would, and explained that it was too small for an acknowledgement. It was about crossing borders, the line.

Forensic oceanographers have demonstrated that military and rescue ships knew the migrant boat's position in the left-to-die boat case. The sea must be safer than the land, no matter where it's going. Keeping two lines apart.

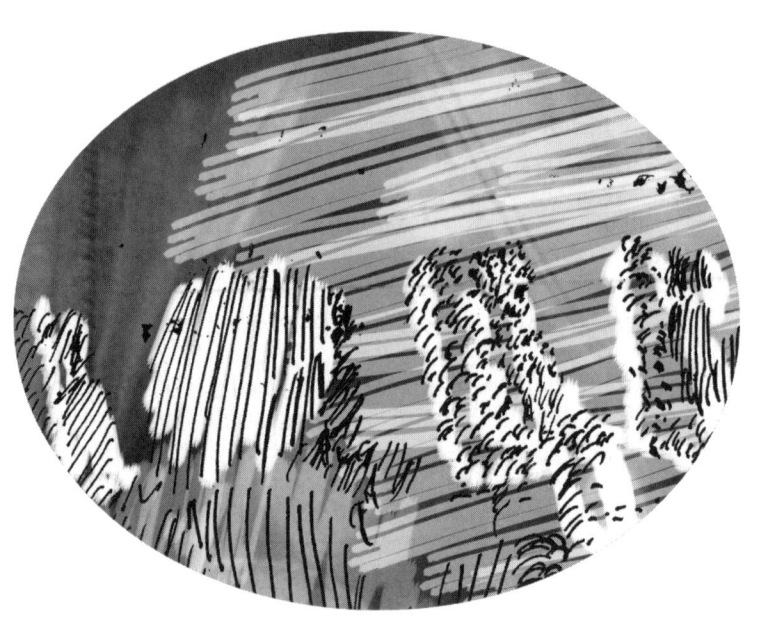

Copenhagen to Stockholm

On the train from Copenhagen
over the bridge and then through Malmö,
the landscape is Scandinoir, every view
a crime scene: Border Control stand
in a circle for their platform briefing,
and in the car park surrounded
by forest, a man in sunglasses
leans against a white car, arms folded,
listening or not to the girl in heels,
cocktail dress, who remonstrates up close;
there's one other car in the car park,
black, and a powder-blue skip, graffiti.

Lunch is a picnic from the hotel breakfast:
bread rolls, cheese slices, boiled eggs, gherkins.
The girl on reception talked like a tape;
you imagine her off duty, out back,
lying down mannequin-style, all elbows
and knees, plugged in, charging up,
her mouth open – closed – open

Georg Rides the U-Bahn

> *Such is his eye in real life, such is the shape of his cheek.*
> —Holbein's caption to The Merchant Georg Gisze, Gemäldegalerie, Berlin

The Brandenburg gate is tumbling in translucent decals
across each window of the Berlin underground train,
dissolving as shallow tunnel gives way to daylit platform.
Its repeated motif deters the graffiti, and foregrounds a man,
as real as his portrait: Georg has slipped from his frame,
dropping his cap of black velvet, his coral silk sleeves.
He's rendered slip-shod, in padded jacket and denim,
and has learned over years how to sit, in stillness, in silence,
in three-quarter profile. He holds his position, his hands
interlock on his lap as we accelerate, brake in a cycle of light
and dark. He has swapped Hanseatic trade for austerity.
No symbols of self hang from the grab rails or shine
from grey vinyl, no handwritten bills, inkstands or seals,
betrothal carnations, the tick of a clock. He's cut his hair
short, and his unpainted eye is giving back less, doesn't meet
mine to demand, have you finished your looking?
Holbein, I observe him the harder because of your claim.
His eye *in real life*, the shape of his cheek, are criss-crossing
the city, jumping the lines between generations and borders.
You're cleaning your brushes: hand him a ticket as he alights
from your easel, his features a permit for infinite transit.

CLAIRE COLLISON

Thirty-Eight Thousand Feet

These days you are leaky with joy –
the malachite ponds are enough
to set you off.

You twist in your seat,
blink damp eyes over fields
shaped by inheritance,

away from the girl sitting next to you,
who has never flown, and who squeals
¡Que chulo! ¡Que guay!

You have the window seat, but try
to share the oval of wonder with her –

Lean over!
Take pictures on your Smartphone!
Look! Snow!

Today you are slathered in airport unguents;
you are age-defying and light-headed:
you love the stewardess's French pleat.

You want to tell the girl in her distressed
Union Jack tee shirt:

stash these glowy clouds; memorise this light.
It is always like this up here – up here
you could believe in God –

but she has put on her headphones
and is studying her itinerary:

on Wednesday she will visit Greenwich;
Thursday, the Horse Guards Parade.

Below, a car park shimmers
like Candy Crush.

Red-eye

We are allocated two blue standard seats
and no window, so as the plane begins
its roaring run at the sky, we can only imagine
the cold grey lines and blinking lights,
the clouds behind the walls of plate and rivet.

Outside the private corridor where we sit
in rinsed and re-rinsed air, frostflowers unfurl
between inches of glass. Picture the long dip
of the wing, the nose's tilt up to the moon –
just like the fox we saw one midnight, who tilted
his nose to rest on a star, then streaked for home.

The Crow and the Dove Take Your Shape

I try to walk you out of mind but the lane
from my cottage is a bridge to Brooklyn. Bare networks
of winter trees are steel struts from which a man once fell.
The jackdaw in the cedar eyeballs me, wears your flat-top.
The stile's stubbled wood, hand in my hand.

I try to walk you out of mind but birds are sirens
rising from ferns at my footfall. In the abandoned dovecote
your every white shirt is neatly folded. Clouds over Chalk Hill
are laundered sheets in that Manhattan hotel – threadbare
like memory worn thin in places.

You're a caw inside my brain, a wing-beat pulse.
The crow who foretells rain. After rain, the homecoming dove.

Uptown

The day before, we'd looped
uptown Manhattan in the rain –
mouths muffled with scarves,

hats pulled low, steam obscuring
the view so we had no choice
but to believe the tour guide

when he told us we'd passed
the spot where John Lennon was shot,
that the Guggenheim was to our left

and the Met to our right. We stayed
on the bus all day, hoping to see
the things we'd missed, looping back

to when Broadway was Native American
Territory, a trail through oak-tulip forests,
or at least until the morning we'd arrived,

choosing to eat breakfast in that small deli,
eggs over easy, tepid coffee, your silence
looping me back to that day in the rain.

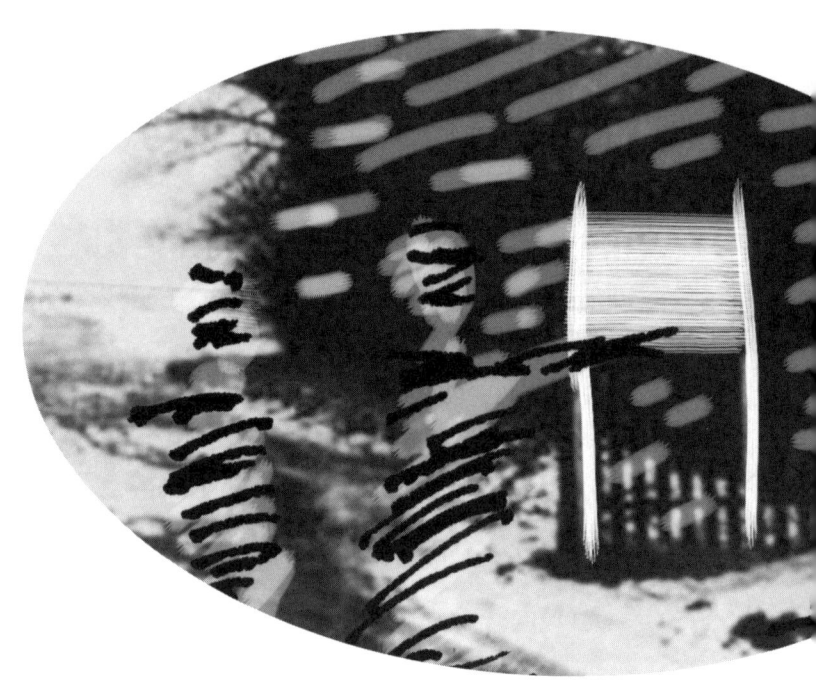

BAIBA BIČOLE

Walking

Against the umbrella, the rhythm of even
                                      raindrops:
minimalism, Philip Glass playing
                              the piano;
in the greenness of grass, trees, bushes,
fauvist and German expressionist
                              maximalism,
but Philip Glass continues to play,
the raindrops, to rain evenly –
I think about the ticking of clocks,
heartbeats, and fears in thick green grass, hidden
and uneven.

**TRANSLATED FROM LATVIAN
BY BITITE VINKLERS**

Portrait of my father as Joseph Cornell

I picture you striding from your digs on Edgware Road
to plunder the curio-sellers on Flask Walk for tin-toy
Aston Martins and books on rare birds and maps
of constellations and jazz recordings
rare as hen's teeth.

Sometimes you load your Balda bellows-camera
with 6x6 Kodak Ektachrome and hike to Piccadilly
to wait under Eros for the perfect alignment:
Red Routemaster jostled by black Hackney cab
de Havilland Flamingo mail-plane overhead

and in that moment you click and you capture
the machines in the saturated colour
spreading from the Coca-Cola billboard, sliding
from the top-end corner of Balloon Street
wrapping around the west end of the Circus

to meet Theatreland. You encounter parrot-bright
streetboys looking for trade, sight-seers clustered in starling gaggles,
commuters on their evening murmurations – all brush past you
unseeing. You catch them in your Ziess Ikon shutter then hop
on the open platform of the number 6 bus westbound

and later, in your workroom – its desk piled with the detritus
of your day job at the Aerodrome (blueprints for bi-planes,
mechanics of gravity, the formula for flight) – you will coax
these birds from the folding box of light and shadows
and give them sanctuary.

Return

Light is greying earlier, fewer leaves
on trees. I'm ravelling up

the route with my back to where I'm going,
as if being dragged. All the way there

station on station and all the way back
reversing their order. I didn't notice the tall

mine-stacks, nor realise that sometimes
they lock the carriages at stops.

The man in the next seat reads the safety leaflet,
looks for the alarms. Easy to feel lost

in the fog beyond the window, losing
the way, losing track

like my grandmother forgetting not to make
two cups of tea. She always said *only ever*

buy return tickets. All I need do
is sit and wait till I get there.

If You Lived Here You'd Be Home By Now

I woke on a bullet train
to find my long-dead mother
had made an investment
in twelve baby sharks
that knifed around our old carp pool.

Outside the train the typhoon raged.
I saw my mother in the hills
telling frantic trees these sharks
would grow into my fame.
Here is her house, they'll say,

The House of Frantic Stepping.
Of course I tried to talk her down,
but how can one reason with a shade?
My mother glared back at me,
drenched in tradition.

A tunnel for a mile, two miles, then out.
The left window revealed Guangxi's jade foothills,
the right window the gloom of the M25.
My mother fed her sharks our heirlooms by hand.
Trucks hauled our past towards a future.

The Blue

I hear her behind me, *beautiful, beautiful,*
on days like this, when the blue seems endless,
when the train belts south for hours and hours,
when cooling towers simmer like contented kettles,
when it's winter, deep winter, but you see the twigged nests
of trees and think of life not death, when the further south you go
the more things go on living, when in a split-second
you pass a field of peasant farmers unearthing green vegetables
from the soil, and watch one lift his face towards your train
and imagine him smiling or sighing, no facemask today, maybe humming
some sonorous peasant song, one of those you've heard on the metro, at night;
when the sun glints on the pylons, that seem to hold their cables a little looser,
on days like this, where you can race the vapour trails of planes,

when the woman behind you takes picture after picture, for eight whole hours, pictures of edgelands, pylons, girders, half-finished skyscrapers, traffic jams, brown fields, iced-over streams, construction vehicles, the sky, rubbish bags on a platform, trees, a hamlet's hillside pagoda, muttering beautiful, piaoliang, beautiful, a maple tree, beautiful, a roadside quarry, a glass factory, the sky, the sun shining on grey stones, ice floating down the Yangtze, junk boats full of coal, a school, a tree full of egrets, a lonesome bull, more pylons, piaoliang, the sky, smoke rising from a bonfire, an abandoned town, a colourful village, a fishing lake, shipping crates, a countryside driving school, a JCB perched on a mound of rocks, a pipeline, a yellow farmhouse, a white stone hut in a brown field, six hay bales, beautiful, the blue, beautiful, then a sudden tunnel, her own startled reflection, then out again into the blue, its heavy and astonishing blast, like bells, bells that have just stopped ringing, on days like these, days like these when it feels like we're winning.

In Dyeliva

The drivers working the main station
have stories of worse years, but still the cold
stupefies outsiders.

In letters from his 1890 visit
the diarist and prospector James Hampton
notes the solemn, long-cheeked aspect
of local women
       (implacable as the climate)
and some peculiarities of the dialect.

Approached by plane at night
a thread of light, bodying through low cloud
is the city's first suggestion.
This was the trade road
that bound the old capital to the coast.

On biting days
locals say it is cold *to the roots*
by which they mean both the roots of trees
and of teeth.

La Pive

I've often transplanted it
from Valais woods to foreign forests:
my grandmother's word for a fircone.

The Académie française would scowl
at this word used by Swiss *paysans*.
Even the dictionary shows me its *correcteur*

then tells me that in France, *le pive*
is a bullfinch, or slang for house red.
La pive – the feminine – a dunce.

A peasants' word? Pine is *sapin*
in the most cultured French.
Sappos in earthy Gaulish, crossed with

pinus: the imperious Latin stem.
I cultivate these branches
and plantings of the tongue –

can trace *pive* back to Sanskrit,
the scripture of the Vedas –
its taproot: *pit*, meaning resin.

My grandmother showed me how summer
unlocks the bracts of *pives*, loosing a swarm
of pips, each with its single wing.

She'd point to a nurse-log, burdened with seedlings,
or a hacked stump in a grove
caulking its wound, live at the roots.

Gods, Cabo de São Vicente, Portugal

We gods sometimes travel to
the region in throngs as large as
flocks of migrant birds, arriving in
spring with nightingales and
orioles and other sweet passerines.

> Battalions of us move along the
> coast, following griffons, white
> storks and black storks, Egyptian
> vultures and booted eagles.

A map of our lives would be a
picture of oscillation between
gatherings. Hubbub. Invisible
crowds of us, all jostling for
morsels of recognition.

> Only when we take refuge
> from seeing and being seen
> on the westernmost point of
> consciousness, do we feel anything
> close to peace.

GEORGE DAVID CLARK

Little Blue Truck

The sun was low. The redbuds glowed.
We drove and drove and drove and drove

from Little Rock past Statesboro
and all that way the redbuds glowed.

Then slower on a red-dirt road
we passed a lake and one more grove

of redbuds, glowing – sun was low –
and still we drove and drove and drove.

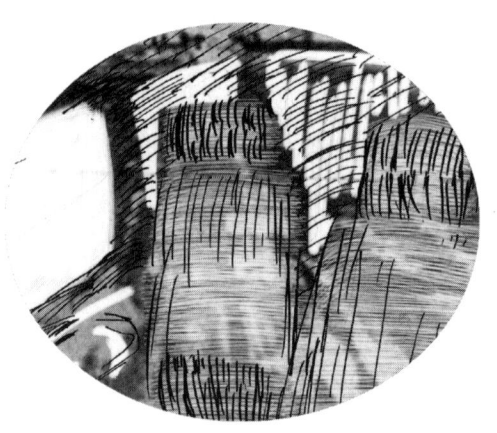

ACKNOWLEDGEMENTS

'South' and 'Family Reunion, March 2001', by Zayneb Allak, were both previously published in her collection, *Keine Angst* (New Walk Editions, 2017).

'West Highland', by Sharon Black, was previously published in *Agenda* (summer 2016).

'Reading the Water', by Nancy Campbell, was previously published in her collection *Disko Bay* (Enitharmon, 2015).

'Little Blue Truck', by George David Clark, was previously published in the *Pittsburgh Poetry Review* (Vol. 5, 2017).

'Thirty-eight thousand feet', by Claire Collison, was previously published in the *Templar Poetry Anthology* (2016).

'The Crow and the Dove Take Your Shape', by Anna Kisby, was previously published in *154* (Live Canon, 2016).

'Men in Water', by Andy Eaton, was previously published in *Poetry Ireland Review* 115 (2015).

'Halfway to Voronezh', by Charlotte Eichler, was previously published by *The Interpreter's House* (2016).

'Empty Quarter', by Rosie Garland, was previously published in the anthology *More Raw Material* (Lucifer Press, 2016).

'Return', by Rebecca Gethin, was previously published in *Brittle Star* (October 2015).

'The Long Flight Home', by Shara Lessley, was previously published in her collection *The Explosive Expert's Wife* (University of Wisconsin Press, 2018).

'A Sight to See' and 'Square Dancing the Adriatic', by Colleen J. McElroy, were both previously published in her collection *Travelling Music* (Story Line Press, 1998).

'Postcard', by Fiona Moore, was previously published in *Poetry London* (2011) and her pamphlet *The Only Reason for Time* (HappenStance Press, 2013).

'France', by Miranda Peake, was previously published in *Poetry News* (2016).

'The romance of men in boats', by Miranda Peake, was previously published on the Poetry School website, as part of the Primers programme 2016.

'In Dyeliva', by Peter Surkov, was previously published on thisisyours.org (2012).

'Beijing', by David Tait, was previously published in his collection *Three Dragon Day* (smith|doorstop, 2015).

'[Watford Gap]', by Andrew Taylor, was previously published in *In The Company of Ghosts: The Poetics of the Motorway* (erbacce-Press, 2012).

'Travelling on the 10:21 with Tom Hardy', by Maria Taylor, was previously published in her collection *Instructions For Making Me* (HappenStance, 2016).

'Чайка (Chaika)', by Alex Toms, was previously published in the anthology *Free-fall: Art from Poetry and Poetry from Art* (2017).

'Epicentres' and 'Sleeper', by Rory Waterman, were both previously published in *Sarajevo Roses* (Carcanet, 2017).

ABOUT THE EDITORS

Sarah Jackson is the author of *Pelt* (Bloodaxe, 2012), which won the Seamus Heaney Award and was longlisted for the Guardian First Book Award, and *Tactile Poetics: Touch and Contemporary Writing* (Edinburgh University Press, 2015). She is an AHRC Leadership Fellow, a BBC/AHRC New Generation Thinker and Senior Lecturer at Nottingham Trent University.

Tim Youngs is Professor of English at Nottingham Trent University and the author and editor of several books on travel writing. His poems have appeared in many magazines, including *Magma*, *The Interpreter's House*, *Poetry Salzburg Review* and *Stride*. His debut pamphlet, *Touching Distance*, was published by Five Leaves in 2017.

ABOUT THE AUTHORS

Zayneb Allak has travelled and worked all over the world. At the time of going to press, she's daydreaming about travels in Colombia. In her real life she's a lecturer in Creative Writing at Edge Hill University. Her debut pamphlet, *Keine Angst*, was published by New Walk Editions in 2017.

Baiba Bičole, a prominent Latvian poet since the 1970s, was born in Latvia but left as a refugee during World War II and has lived in the United States since 1950. She is the author of six collections of poetry and has received major Latvian literary awards.

Sharon Black is originally from Glasgow but now lives in the Cévennes mountains of France, having previously lived in Japan after catching the travelling bug in her late teens. She has two collections: *To Know Bedrock* (Pindrop, 2011) and *The Art of Egg* (Two Ravens, 2015). www.sharonblack.co.uk

Jeanette Burton has an MA in Creative Writing from Nottingham Trent University and teaches English at a sixth-form College in Nottingham. This is her first published poem.

Nancy Campbell's books include *Disko Bay* (shortlisted for the Forward Prize for Best First Collection 2016) and *How To Say 'I Love You' In Greenlandic* (winner of the Birgit Skiöld Award). Her memoir, *The Library of Ice*, will be published by Scribner in 2018. She is currently the Canal Laureate.

George David Clark's collection *Reveille* won the 2015 Miller Williams Prize and his new work can be found in *Agni, The Georgia Review, The Gettysburg Review, The Southern Review* and elsewhere. He edits the journal *32 Poems* and lives with his wife and their four young children in Washington, Pennsylvania.

Claire Collison is a writer, visual artist, breast cancer survivor and artist-in-residence at The Women's Art Library. Her work has been published widely. She came second in the Resurgence Prize and second in the Hippocrates Prize. Claire performs a life modelling monologue, 'Truth is Beauty'.

Anna Kisby lives in Devon, UK. Her poetry is widely published in magazines and anthologies, she won the BBC Proms Poetry competition 2016, and she was commended in the Faber New Poets Scheme 2015-16. Her debut pamphlet *All the Naked Daughters* is published by Against the Grain Press (2017).

Jo Dixon is a poet and critic living in Nottingham. Her poems have appeared in a range of poetry publications, including *New Walk, The Interpreter's House* and *Furies* (For Books' Sake). Her debut poetry pamphlet, *A Woman in the Queue*, was published by Melos Press in 2016.

Andy Eaton was born in California and raised throughout the United States. He lives in Belfast and teaches in Oxford. His poems are published widely in places such as *Copper Nickel, Ploughshares* and *The Yale Review*. A pamphlet, *Sprung Nocturne*, was published by the Lifeboat Press in 2016.

Charlotte Eichler's poems have appeared in magazines such as *Blackbox Manifold, PN Review, The Rialto* and *Stand*. In 2017, *Poetry London* awarded Charlotte a year's mentoring with Vahni Capildeo. Her first pamphlet, *Their Lunar Language*, is coming out with Valley Press in 2018.

Rosie Garland is a novelist, poet and singer with post-punk band The March Violets. With a passion for language nurtured by public libraries, her poems have appeared in *Bare Fiction, New Welsh Review, The Rialto* and elsewhere. She won the inaugural Mslexia Novel Competition.

Rebecca Gethin lives on Dartmoor and has published two pamphlets, two collections, and two novels. Her poems have been published widely, and she runs a Poetry School seminar in Plymouth. www.rebeccagethin.wordpress.com

Rich Goodson has been teaching migrant and refugee teenagers for the last twenty-one years. His debut, *Mr Universe* (Eyewear), was a Poetry Book Society Pamphlet Choice in 2017.

Susannah Hart is a London-based poet whose work has been widely published in magazines and online. She is on the board of *Magma Poetry* and her first collection is due to be published by Live Canon in 2018. She's also a keen traveller who loves learning different languages.

Fiona Larkin's poems appear in journals and anthologies, including *Magma, The North, Envoi* and *Under the Radar*, and *Best New British and Irish Poets 2018* (Eyewear). She has an MA in Creative Writing from Royal Holloway.

Shara Lessley is the author of *Two-Headed Nightingale* and *The Explosive Expert's Wife*. A former Stegner Fellow at Stanford University, her awards include a National Endowment for the Arts Fellowship and Colgate University's O'Connor Fellowship. She co-edited *A Poem's Country: Place & Poetic Practice*.

Nick Littler is a poet and songwriter from Exeter, now living in Cardiff, where he is trying and failing to learn Welsh. His poem 'Frank' will appear in the forthcoming Emma Press anthology of poems about Britain.

Lila Matsumoto's publications include *Urn & Drum* (Shearsman), *Soft Troika* (If a Leaf Falls Press) and *Allegories from my Kitchen* (Sad Press). She teaches poetry at the University of Nottingham and co-runs *Front Horse*, a magazine and performance night of poetry, music, and art.

Colleen J. McElroy lives in Seattle, Washington. Her collection *Queen of the Ebony Isles* won an American Book Award in 1985. Her collection *Blood Memory* was a finalist for the 2017 Paterson Poetry Prize. Many of her poems have been translated into languages including Russian, Italian, Arabic, and Serbo-Croatian.

Jane McKie's most recent poetry collection is *Kitsune* (Cinnamon Press, 2015), and her most recent pamphlet is *From the Wonder Book of Would You Believe It?* (Mariscat Press, 2016). She is a Lecturer in Creative Writing at the University of Edinburgh.

Fiona Moore's first collection *The Distal Point* will be published by HappenStance Press in July 2018. Her pamphlet *Night Letter* was shortlisted for the 2016 Michael Marks Awards. She is co-editing *Magma* 72 on climate change. She used to help edit *The Rialto*, blogs occasionally at *Displacement*, and writes reviews.

Miranda Peake is a poet and artist based in London. Her poems have been published in magazines and journals, including *Ambit, Bare Fiction, Magma, The Moth, Oxford Poetry* and *The Rialto*. In 2014 she won the Mslexia Poetry Competition. She is a member of the Hornet Press Poetry Collective.

Cheryl Pearson lives and writes in Manchester. Her poems have appeared or are forthcoming in publications including *The Guardian, The High Window, Under The Radar* and *The Compass*. She has twice been nominated for a Pushcart Prize. Her first full poetry collection, *Oysterlight*, was published in 2017.

Ilse Pedler lives and works as a veterinary surgeon in Saffron Walden. She often finds that poems come to her in the car between visits and ends up scribbling on bits of paper in lay-bys. Her pamphlet *The Dogs That Chase Bicycle Wheels* won the Mslexia Pamphlet Competition and was published by Seren in 2016.

Yvonne Reddick is a poet and ecopoetry scholar. She has received a Northern Writer's Award, the *Mslexia* Pamphlet Competition, a Hawthornden Fellowship and the Poetry Society's inaugural Peggy Poole Award. Her pamphlet *Translating Mountains* (Seren, 2017) was selected as a favourite pamphlet of the year in the *Times Literary Supplement*.

Andrea Robinson is an artist, writer and printmaker. Her work is inspired by handed-down histories (and her much-travelled ancestors). Recent poems have been published by *Coast to Coast to Coast*, Fair Acre Press, *Smeuse*, *Visual Verse*, and in a sound installation for Protein Dance. www.andrearobinsonartist.co.uk

William Roychowdhury works in international development. He is often in transit. He tries to fit poetry between his job and looking after his two young children. His work has been published in a variety of magazines.

Vicky Sparrow's poems can be found in *Front Horse, datableed* and *Litmus*. Her first pamphlet, *Notes to Selves* (2016), is published by Zarf Editions. She is completing a PhD on the poet-activist Anna Mendelssohn at Birkbeck, and edits reviews for the *Journal of British and Irish Innovative Poetry*.

David Tait's first collection, *Self-Portrait with The Happiness*, won an Eric Gregory Award and was shortlisted for the Fenton Aldeburgh First Collection Prize. His pamphlet *Three Dragon Day* was shortlisted for the Michael Marks Award. His new collection *The AQI* is out in October 2018.

Andrew Taylor has published two collections with Shearsman and has pamphlets with Oystercatcher, Leafe, zimZalla, The Red Ceilings and Stranger Press. www.andrewtaylorpoetry.com

Maria Taylor is a poet and reviewer of Cypriot origin. Her most recent pamphlet, *Instructions for Making Me*, is published by HappenStance Press. Her debut collection, *Melanchrini* (Nine Arches Press), was shortlisted for the Michael Murphy Memorial Prize.

Alex Toms is a mum and trainee pharmacy advisor from Wivenhoe, Essex. Her poems have appeared in, among other places, *Mslexia, Under the Radar* and the Bloodaxe anthology *Hallelujah for 50ft Women*. Her debut collection will be published by Dunlin Press in late 2018. www.alextomspoet.com

Bitite Vinklers is a translator of Latvian folklore and contemporary literature, with work in numerous anthologies and journals, including *The Paris Review, Denver Quarterly* and

Poetry Daily. Recent publications include Knuts Skujenieks, *Seed in Snow: Poems* (BOA Editions, 2016).

Rory Waterman is the author of *Tonight the Summer's Over* (Carcanet, 2013), which was a Poetry Book Society Recommendation, and *Sarajevo Roses* (Carcanet, 2017), as well as two books on twentieth-century poetry. He is a senior lecturer in English, and co-edits the poetry pamphlet series *New Walk Editions*.

Rebecca Violet White is a poet who recently escaped London for a narrowboat in the West Country. Since finishing her Creative Writing Masters at UEA in 2014, she has been published by *Ink, Sweat and Tears*, *For Book's Sake* and *Elbow Room*.

Simon Williams has eight published collections, his latest being a co-authored pamphlet with Susan Taylor, *The Weather House*, published in 2017 by Indigo Dreams. Simon was elected The Bard of Exeter in 2013 and founded the large-format magazine, *The Broadsheet*.

Jeremy Wikeley grew up in Romsey and now lives and works in London, but he used to get the train to Cambridge a lot. His poems, which have appeared in magazines like *The North* and *Magma*, often involve moving from one place to another.

Peter Surkov is a medical student and ex-marketeer. Recent poems have appeared in *Magma*, *The Stockholm Review* and *Envoi*.

Cliff Yates' collections include *Henry's Clock* (winner of the Aldeburgh First Collection Prize), *Frank Freeman's Dancing School* (Salt; Knives Forks & Spoons) and *Jam* (smith|doorstop). He is a former Poetry Society poet-in-residence and the author of *Jumpstart Poetry in the Secondary School*.